# Collins Primary Maths
# Pupil Book 3

## Series Editor: Peter Clarke

Authors: Andrew Edmondson, Elizabeth Jurgensen,
Jeanette Mumford, Sandra Roberts

# Contents

| | patterns and relationships, generalise and predict. Suggest extensions by asking "What if…?" | |
|---|---|---|
| Rapid recall of multiplication and division facts | To find remainders after division<br>To derive quickly doubles of multiples of 100 to 5000<br>(e.g. 3400 × 2) and the corresponding halves (e.g. $\frac{1}{2}$ of 6800) | 36, 42 |
| Understanding multiplication and division/Mental calculation strategies (× and ÷)/Rapid recall of multiplication and division facts/Problems involving "real life" | To round up or down after division, depending on the context<br>To begin to know multiplication facts for the 9 times table<br>To begin to know multiplication facts for the 7 times table<br>To know by heart multiplication facts for 2, 3, 4, 5 and 10 times tables<br>To use known number facts and place value to multiply and divide integers, including by 10 and then 100 (whole number answers) | 37, 38, 39, 40, 43 |
| Pencil and paper procedures (× and ÷)/Checking results of calculations | To develop and refine written methods for TU ÷ U | 44 |
| Fractions and decimals | To begin to use ideas of simple proportion: for example, "one in every…"<br>To recognise the equivalence between the decimal and fraction forms of one half and one quarter and tenths such as 0·3 | 46, 47, 48, 49, 50 |
| Understanding addition and subtraction/Rapid recall of addition and subtraction facts/Mental calculation strategies (+ and −)/Checking results of calculations | Consolidate understanding of relationships between addition and subtraction | 51 |
| Measures: (Time)/Problems involving measures (time)/Making decisions | To read simple timetables and use this year's calendar | 54, 55 |
| Organising and interpreting data | To solve a problem by collecting quickly, organising, representing and interpreting data in tables, charts, graphs and diagrams, including those generated by a computer, for example:<br>Venn diagrams (two criteria) | 56, 57, 58, 59, 60, 61, 62, 63, 64 |

## Acknowledgements

The publisher would like to thank the following for their valuable comments and advice when trialling and reviewing Collins Primary Maths ⧨ materials.

Concetta Cino – Barrow Hill Junior School, London
Mrs B Crank – Heron Hill County Primary, Kendal, Cumbria
Elizabeth Fairhead – Puttenham C of E School, Guildford, Surrey
Mrs D Kelley – Green Lane First School, Bradford
Alison Lowe – Goddard Park Primary School, Swindon
Sarah Nower – Watchetts Junior School, Camberley, Surrey
Miss M Richards – Birchfield Primary School, Birmingham
Mrs S Simco – Heron Hill County Primary, Kendal, Cumbria
Janice Turk – Sacred Heart Junior School, London
Chris Wilson – Woodville School, Leatherhead, Surrey

# Number tracks

## Refresher

1 What is the red digit worth?

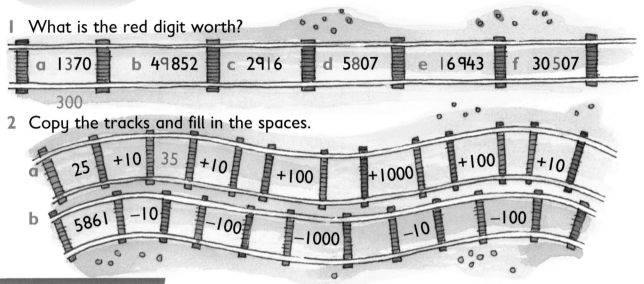

a 1370   b 49852   c 2916   d 5807   e 16943   f 30507

300

2 Copy the tracks and fill in the spaces.

a 25 +10 35 +10 +100 +1000 +100 +10

b 5861 −10 −100 −1000 −10 −100

## Practice

1 Copy the tracks and fill in the spaces.

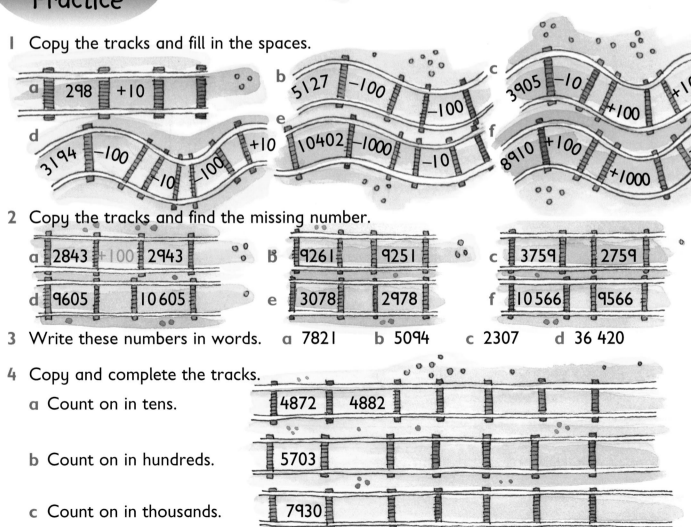

a 298 +10

b 5127 −100 −100

c 3905 −10 +100 +100

d 3194 −100 −10 −100 +10

e 10402 −1000 −10

f 8910 +100 +1000 −10

2 Copy the tracks and find the missing number.

a 2843 +100 2943   b 9261 9251   c 3759 2759

d 9605 10605   e 3078 2978   f 10566 9566

3 Write these numbers in words.   a 7821   b 5094   c 2307   d 36 420

4 Copy and complete the tracks.

a Count on in tens. 4872 4882

b Count on in hundreds. 5703

c Count on in thousands. 7930

5

# All in order!

## Refresher

**1** Write these numbers in order, smallest to largest.

  a  [ 4870 ] [ 9350 ] [ 2164 ]          b  [ 8142 ] [ 4182 ] [ 305 ] [ 2841 ]

  c  [ 2643 ] [ 3462 ] [ 4632 ]          d  [ 9406 ] [ 4900 ] [ 694 ] [ 490 ]

**2** Multiply these numbers by 100.

  a [ 79 ]          b [ 400 ]          c [ 259 ]          d [ 1307 ]

  e [ 5926 ]        f [ 8000 ]         g [ 7900 ]         h [ 1050 ]

## Practice

**1** Write these numbers in order, smallest to largest.

  a  [ 6843 ] [ 9683 ] [ 6983 ]          b  [ 3500 ] [ 5300 ] [ 3050 ] [ 5033 ]

  c  [ 2509 ] [ 2905 ] [ 5209 ]          d  [ 7144 ] [ 523 ] [ 7414 ] [ 325 ] [ 97 ]

**2** Put these weights in order, lightest to heaviest.

  a  805 g  508 g  850 g          b  4613 g  4136 g  6413 g

  c  995 g  599 g  1459 g  950 g          d  2244 g  4224 g  2424 g

**3** Change these amounts to pence.

  a £7          b £36          c £592          d £825          e £4500

**4** Change these lengths to centimetres.

  a 20 m          b 504 m          c 3000 m          d 250 m          e 9010 m

# Sweet estimates

## Refresher

1  Estimate the amount of milkshake to the nearest 100 ml.

2  Round these numbers to the nearest 10.

a 134    b 75    c 852    d 396    e 605    f 992    g 4255

3  Round each number in question 2 to the nearest 100.

## Practice

1  Estimate the number of sweets in each jar.
   The number beside each jar shows how many sweets it contains when full.

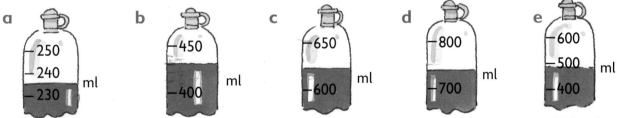

2  Estimate the amounts of strawberry syrup to the nearest 10 ml.

a
250
240
ml
230

b
450
ml
400

c
650
ml
600

d
800
ml
700

e
600
500  ml
400

3  For each of the bottles in question 2, estimate the amount to the nearest 100 ml.

4  Copy this number line.

0                                                                                    100
|_____|

Mark these numbers on the number line.
50   25   75   90   30   60   10

7

# Use your facts!

## Refresher

Choose two calculations that go together, one from each
bucket. Then write the answers to both calculations.

6 + 2
4 + 3
8 – 3
5 + 4
9 + 3
13 – 5
7 + 6
12 – 4
9 + 5
14 – 6
4 + 9

130 – 50
80 – 30
70 + 60
50 + 40
40 + 90
120 – 40
90 + 30
40 + 30
140 – 60
60 + 20
90 + 50

## Practice

Choose three calculations that go together, one from each bucket.
Then write the answers to all three calculations.

8 + 7
8 + 8
18 – 9
9 + 7
7 + 5
16 – 7
6 + 6
15 – 8
12 + 5
14 – 3

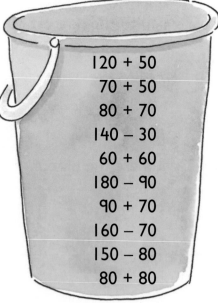

120 + 50
70 + 50
80 + 70
140 – 30
60 + 60
180 – 90
90 + 70
160 – 70
150 – 80
80 + 80

1200 + 500
800 + 800
900 + 700
1400 – 300
1500 – 800
800 + 700
700 + 500
1600 – 700
1800 – 900
600 + 600

# Tortoise addition

## Refresher

Choose a number from each tortoise and make ten addition calculations.

**⌐Example⌐**
36 + 20 = 56

## Practice

1 Choose a number from each tortoise and make ten addition calculations.

2 Work out these subtraction calculations.

a 372 − 40                          b 367 − 30
c 684 − 60                          d 792 − 70
e 841 − 20                          f 958 − 50
g 586 − 70                          h 892 − 80
i 465 − 40                          j 773 − 60

# What's the jump?

## Refresher

Work out what jump each kangaroo needs to make to reach the next multiple of 100.

a 36 → 100  b 24 → 100  c 75 → 100  d 83 → 100  e 62 → 100

36 + 64 = 100

f 57 → 100  g 156 → 100  h 148 → 100  i 231 → 100  j 265 → 100

## Practice

Work out the missing steps.

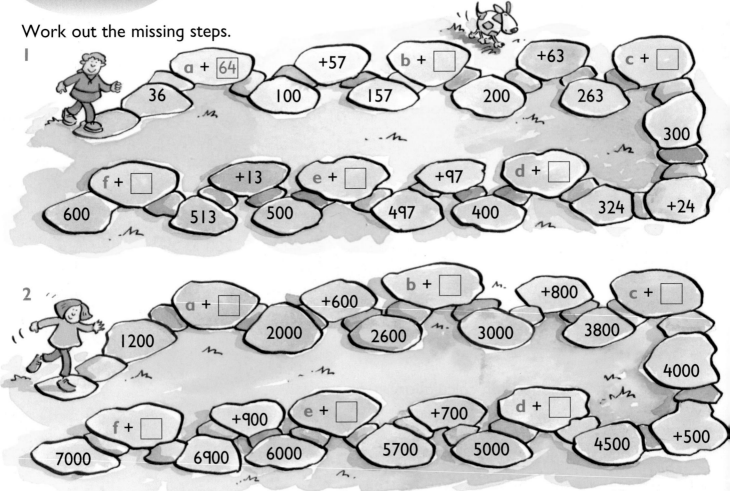

**1**

36 — a + 64 → 100 — +57 → 157 — b + □ → 200 — +63 → 263 — c + □ → 300

600 — f + □ → 513 — +13 → 500 — e + □ → 497 — +97 → 400 — d + □ → 324 — +24 → 300

**2**

1200 — a + □ → 2000 — +600 → 2600 — b + □ → 3000 — +800 → 3800 — c + □ → 4000

7000 — f + □ → 6900 — +900 → 6000 — e + □ → 5700 — +700 → 5000 — d + □ → 4500 — +500 → 4000

# Space calculations

Write down four calculations for each spaceship. Start with the number on the main part and add or subtract the digits on each leg.

## Refresher

1
234
+5  +2  –3  –4

2
253
+6  +5  –3  –2

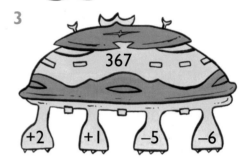

3
367
+2  +1  –5  –6

4
456
+5  +7  –8  –7

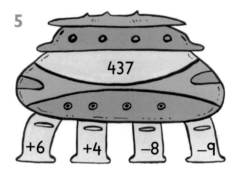

5
437
+6  +4  –8  –9

## Practice

1
627
+7  +9  –8  –9

2
1354
+7  +9  –6  –7

3
800
–5  –3  –7  –8

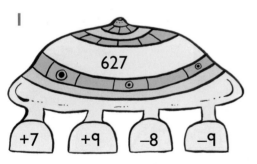

4
3465
+9  +7  –8  –6

5
5686
+7  +5  –9  –7

6
7000
–8  –5  –1  –7

# Number facts

## Refresher

Work out these calculations.

a 24 + 45 = ☐    b 32 + 57 = ☐    c 28 + 61 = ☐    d 72 + 25 = ☐    e 84 + 16 = ☐

f 87 − 43 = ☐    g 95 − 52 = ☐    h 83 − 32 = ☐    i 79 − 55 = ☐    j 68 − 26 = ☐

## Practice

- You will need a partner to work with.
- You and your partner each choose a number from the hundred square.
- Use the two numbers to make a calculation.
- Work it out and check to see if you have the same answer.
- Make up ten addition and ten subtraction calculations.

| 1 | 2 | 3 | 4 | 5 | 6 | 7 | 8 | 9 | 10 |
|---|---|---|---|---|---|---|---|---|---|
| 11 | 12 | 13 | 14 | 15 | 16 | 17 | 18 | 19 | 20 |
| 21 | 22 | 23 | 24 | 25 | 26 | 27 | 28 | 29 | 30 |
| 31 | 32 | 33 | 34 | 35 | 36 | 37 | 38 | 39 | 40 |
| 41 | 42 | 43 | 44 | 45 | 46 | 47 | 48 | 49 | 50 |
| 51 | 52 | 53 | 54 | 55 | 56 | 57 | 58 | 59 | 60 |
| 61 | 62 | 63 | 64 | 65 | 66 | 67 | 68 | 69 | 70 |
| 71 | 72 | 73 | 74 | 75 | 76 | 77 | 78 | 79 | 80 |
| 81 | 82 | 83 | 84 | 85 | 86 | 87 | 88 | 89 | 90 |
| 91 | 92 | 93 | 94 | 95 | 96 | 97 | 98 | 99 | 100 |

# Racing addition

Write the calculations out vertically then work out the answers.

**~Example~**

a

|   | 1 | 4 | 3 |
|---|---|---|---|
| + | 1 | 2 | 4 |
|   |   |   |   |

## Refresher

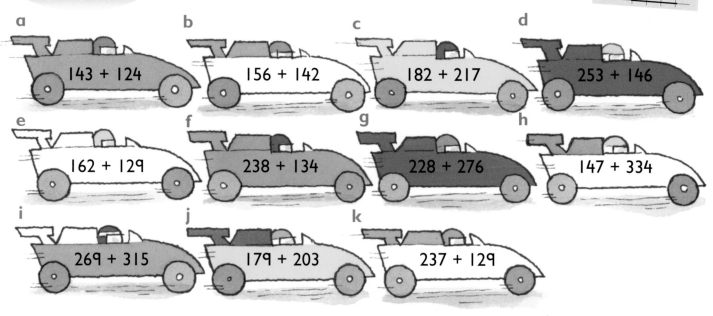

a   143 + 124

b   156 + 142

c   182 + 217

d   253 + 146

e   162 + 129

f   238 + 134

g   228 + 276

h   147 + 334

i   269 + 315

j   179 + 203

k   237 + 129

## Practice

a   264 + 238

b   217 + 327

c   254 + 236

d   309 + 255

e   428 + 239

f   282 + 251

g   353 + 262

h   271 + 245

i   431 + 380 + 146

j   362 + 475 + 206

k   273 + 167 + 318

l   162 + 258 + 167

# Shop calculations

## Refresher

**Example**

a
```
  2 4 3
+ 3 1 8
```

1 Write these calculations vertically and then work them out.

a  243 + 318 = ☐          b  436 + 125 = ☐

c  349 + 203 = ☐          d  237 + 214 = ☐

e  346 + 138 = ☐          f  264 + 352 = ☐

g  383 + 121 = ☐          h  475 + 252 = ☐

i  286 + 281 = ☐          j  198 + 421 = ☐

## Practice

1 Choose two items from the shelf and add up their cost. Do this 10 times.

a          b          c          d          e          f

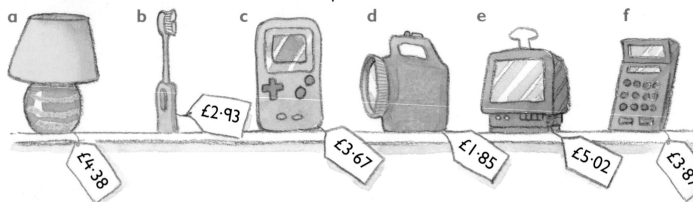

£2·93     £3·67     £1·85     £5·02     £3·8?     £4·38

2 Solve the problem.
   Lee has £2·38. Ruth has £1·56 more than Lee.
   a How much does Ruth have?
   b How much do they have altogether?

# Boat calculations

Write the calculations vertically, then work out the answers.

**Example**

$$
\begin{array}{r}
2\ 3\ 5 \\
-\ 1\ 2\ 3 \\
\hline
3\ 1\ 2 \\
\end{array}
$$

## Refresher

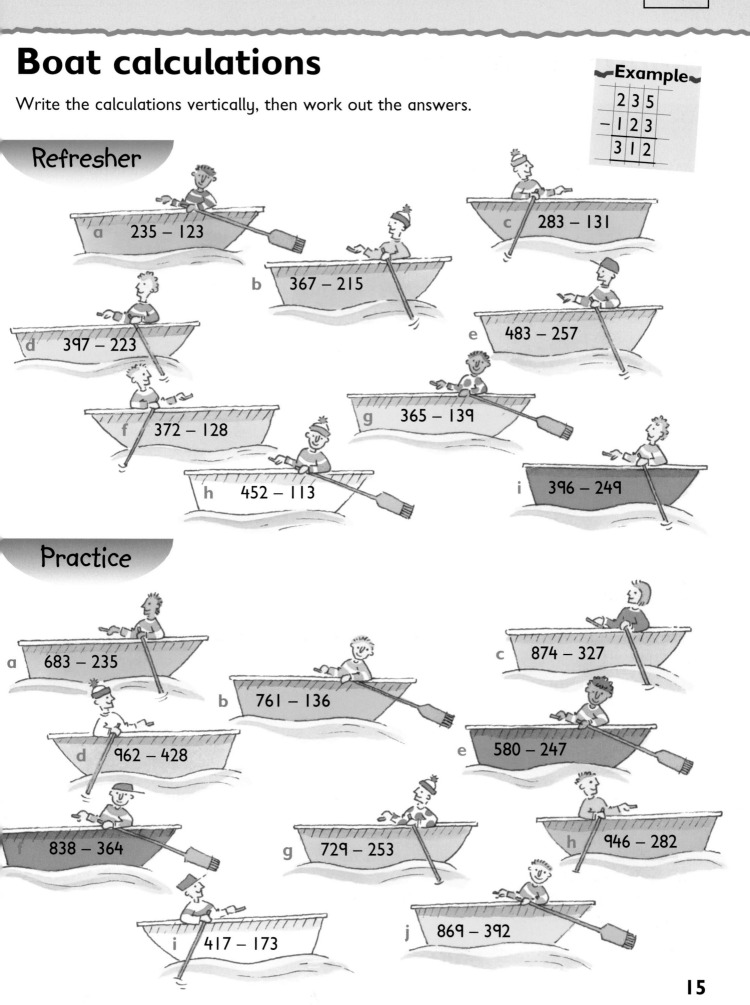

a  235 – 123

b  367 – 215

c  283 – 131

d  397 – 223

e  483 – 257

f  372 – 128

g  365 – 139

h  452 – 113

i  396 – 249

## Practice

a  683 – 235

b  761 – 136

c  874 – 327

d  962 – 428

e  580 – 247

f  838 – 364

g  729 – 253

h  946 – 282

i  417 – 173

j  869 – 392

# Column subtraction

**Example**

$$
\begin{array}{r}
3\ 6\ 2 \\
-\ 1\ 2\ 6 \\
\hline
\end{array}
$$

## Refresher

1  Write these calculations vertically and then work them out.

a  362 − 126 = ☐

b  281 − 138 = ☐

c  293 − 149 = ☐

d  364 − 217 = ☐

e  475 − 238 = ☐

f  328 − 182 = ☐

g  237 − 171 = ☐

h  349 − 193 = ☐

2  Now work out these subtraction calculations in your head. Just write down the answers.

a  105 − 98 = ☐

b  203 − 194 = ☐

c  307 − 295 = ☐

d  206 − 199 = ☐

e  304 − 297 = ☐

f  401 − 393 = ☐

g  302 − 292 = ☐

h  405 − 394 = ☐

## Practice

1  Write out these calculations vertically and then work them out.

a  726 − 247 = ☐

b  634 − 158 = ☐

c  573 − 396 = ☐

d  841 − 482 = ☐

e  460 − 194 = ☐

f  932 − 674 = ☐

g  703 − 436 = ☐

h  627 − 388 = ☐

2  Now work out these subtraction calculations in your head. Just write down the answers.

a  4003 − 3997 = ☐

b  2009 − 1995 = ☐

c  5006 − 4992 = ☐

d  3008 − 2999 = ☐

e  1009 − 991 = ☐

f  7002 − 6998 = ☐

g  8001 − 7993 = ☐

h  9004 − 8994 = ☐

# Money problems

Work out the answers to the problems. Write down the calculation/s you did to work out the answers.

## Refresher

a I wish I had a £100, but I only have £37. How much more do I need?

b My friend and I sorted 150 stickers into two piles. 70 were in one pile. How many were in the other?

c My plant has 67 flowers and my sister's has 42. How many more flowers are on my plant?

d Our teacher told us to collect and bring in boxes. I collected 34. My friend forgot to collect any so I gave him 18 of mine. How many did I take into school?

e The bike I wanted cost £200. Then the price went down by £6. How much is it now?

## Practice

a My mum is trying to save £500. She has £438. How much more does she need to reach her target?

b The shop ordered some new shirts to sell. 60 were sold on the first day. "If I can sell 80 shirts tomorrow I will have sold them all," said the shopkeeper. How many shirts did he have to begin with?

c I earned £18 on Monday and £37 on Tuesday. Mum gave me some money and now I have £58. How much did she give me?

d The library van has 700 adult books and 800 children's books. 600 books are lent to local schools. How many books are left in the library van?

e At the school fair, Paula has a "Guess how many sweets in the jar" competition. I guessed 358 and my friend guessed 241. Paula said "Put your guesses together, subtract 125 and you'll know the answer." How many sweets are in the jar?

● Know the equivalent of one half, one quarter, three quarters and one tenth of 1 litre in ml.

Su 4, 1

# Fractions of a litre

## Refresher

1 Copy and complete.

a 1 litre = 500 ml + ___ ml

= ___ ml

b $\frac{1}{2}$ litre = ___ ml + 250 ml

= ___ ml

c $\frac{1}{10}$ litre = ___ ml

d $\frac{1}{4}$ litre = ___ ml

e $\frac{3}{4}$ litre = 500 ml + ___ ml

= ___ ml

## Practice

1 Write true or false for each of these statements.

a 500 ml = $\frac{1}{2}$ of a litre

b $\frac{1}{4}$ of a litre < 200 ml

c 700 ml < $\frac{3}{4}$ of a litre

d 100 ml = 1 litre

e $\frac{1}{10}$ of a litre = 100 ml

f 400 ml > $\frac{1}{2}$ litre

g $\frac{1}{4}$ l + 500 ml > 750 ml

h 800 ml < $\frac{3}{4}$ litre

2 a The carton of orange juice holds ___ ml

b It will fill ___ glasses.

c The bottle of lemonade holds ___ ml

d It will fill ___ beakers

18

# Millilitres more or less

## Refresher

1 Write, to the nearest 10 ml, the amount of liquid in each measuring cylinder.

a      b      c      d      e

## Practice

1 Copy and complete this table.

|   | Liquid in cylinder | Amount added | Total amount |
|---|---|---|---|
| A |   | 300 ml |   |
| B |   | 150 ml |   |
| C |   | 430 ml |   |
| D |   | 190 ml |   |
| E |   | 580 ml |   |

2 Look at the soft drink containers.
  How many millilitres altogether in:
  a 1 can of lemonade and 1 bottle of orange?
  b 1 carton of juice and 1 can of cola?

3 What is the difference in ml between:
  a 1 can of lemonade and 1 carton of juice?
  b 1 bottle of orange and 1 can of cola?

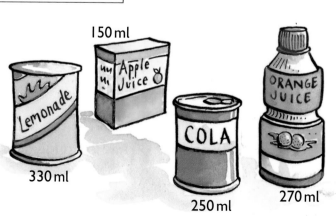

150 ml

330 ml

250 ml

270 ml

19

# Calculating capacities

## Refresher

1 Each container is matched with a cup or a glass .

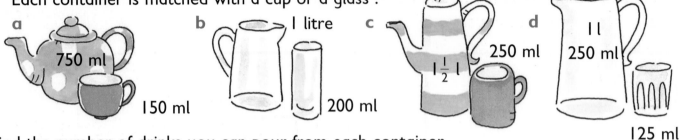

a  750 ml  150 ml

b  1 litre  200 ml

c  1½ l  250 ml

d  1 l  250 ml  125 ml

Find the number of drinks you can pour from each container.
Use the cup or glass beside each container.

## Practice

1 Use the block graph to answer these
questions.

 a Which container has the least capacity?

 b What is the capacity of the coffee pot?

 c How many cups of coffee can you pour?

 d How many cans of cola have the same
   capacity as the bottle of lemonade?

 e You pour 2 glasses of lemonade. How
   much lemonade is left in the bottle?

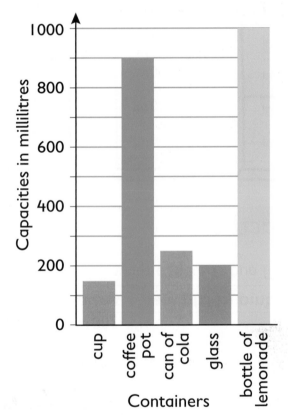

Capacities in millilitres

1000
800
600
400
200
0

cup | coffee pot | can of cola | glass | bottle of lemonade

Containers

2 When cooking rice, you need 3 cups of
water to every cup of rice.
You cook 4 cups of rice.

 a How many cups of water do you need?

 b A cup holds 200 ml. Which saucepan should you use: 2 litres, 3 litres or 10 litres? Why?

3 A bottle of olive oil holds 500 ml.
A tablespoon holds 15 ml.
You measure out 4 tablespoons of oil.
How much oil is left in the bottle?

4 In each 250 ml drink 50 ml is orange squash. The rest is water.
How many litres of water do you need for 10 drinks?

# Fill up in litres

## Refresher

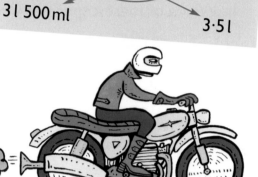

**Example**

3000 ml + 500 ml

3500 ml

$3\frac{1}{2}l$

3 l 500 ml

3·5 l

1 These readings show the amount of fuel in millilitres bought by each motorcyclist.
Write each amount in four different ways.

a 4500 ml

b 5500 ml

c 4250 ml

d 6750 ml

## Practice

1 Copy and complete these petrol pump meter readings for motorcycle sales.

a 4125 ml    4 l 125 ml

b 6427 ml    __ l ___ ml

c ____ ml    7 l 889 ml

d 9050 ml    __ l ___ ml

e ____ ml    8 l 300 ml

f 4997 ml    __ l ___ ml

2 These figures give the engine size in millilitres for each car.

a           b           c           d           e

1044        1395        1589        1616        2250

Copy and complete this table.

| Car | Engine capacity in ml | Rounded to nearest | |
|-----|-----------------------|--------------------|-------------------|
|     |                       | 10 ml | 100 ml |
| a   | 1044                  |       |        |
| b   |                       |       |        |
| c   |                       |       |        |
| d   |                       |       |        |
| e   |                       |       |        |

# Estimating capacities

## Refresher

1 Which of these capacities would you expect each container to hold?

|   |   |   |   |   |
|---|---|---|---|---|
| a | can of lemonade | 30 ml | 330 ml | 3330 ml |
| b | teacup | 500 ml | 250 ml | 150 ml |
| c | teaspoon | 5 ml | 50 ml | 100 ml |
| d | teapot | 0·25 l | 0·5 l | 1 litre |
| e | large saucepan | 500 ml | 1000 ml | 3000 ml |
| f | washing-up basin | 0·75 l | 7·5 l | 75 l |

## Practice

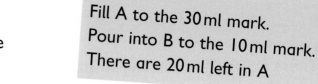

**Example**

a

Fill A to the 30 ml mark.
Pour into B to the 10 ml mark.
There are 20 ml left in A

1 You have these pairs of containers.
Write how you would use them to measure
out the amount of liquid needed.

a
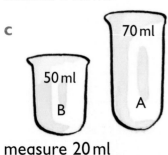
measure 20 ml

b
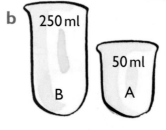
measure 150 ml

c
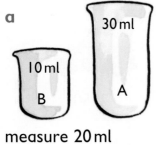
measure 20 ml

d
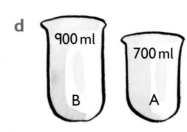
measure 200 ml

2 Use the containers in question c to measure 30 ml.

● Sketch the reflection of a simple shape in a mirror line parallel to one side (all sides parallel of perpendicular to the mirror line)

Su 5, I

# Puzzling reflections

## Refresher

I  Use your mirror to find shapes **a** to **e**.

Use your mirror on this shape to find the shapes a–e.

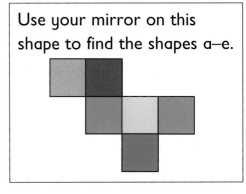

**a**

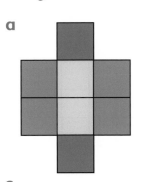

**b**

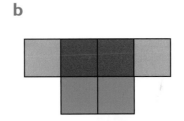

**c**

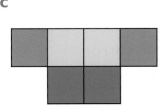

**d**

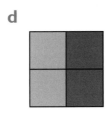

**e**

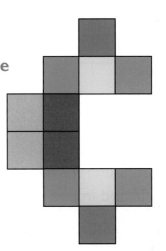

## Practice

I  Use your mirror to find shapes **a** to **g**.

**a**

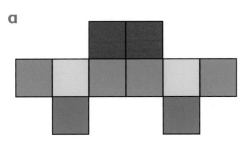

**b**

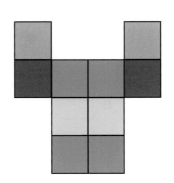

2  These shapes are trickier. Can you find them?

**a**

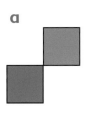

**b**

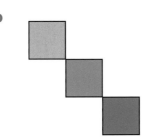

**c**

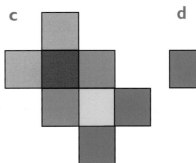

**d**

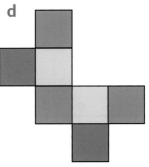

# Reflecting patterns

## Refresher

Copy these patterns on to squared paper. Colour the empty spaces to make them symmetrical.

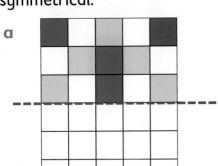

a

b

c

## Practice

Copy these dots and mirror lines on squared paper.
Draw the reflected image of the dots.

**Example**

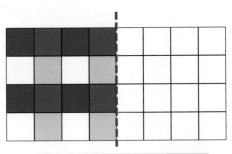

a

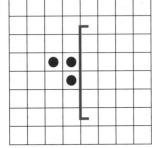

b

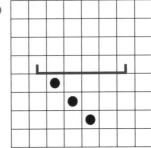

c

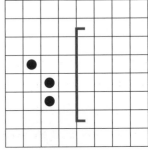

d

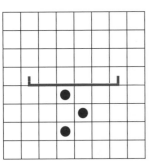

e

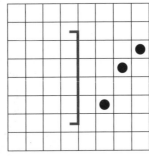

f

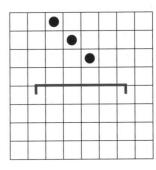

g

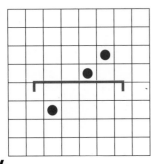

h

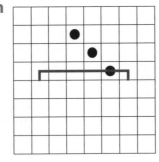

i

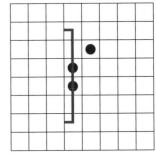

24

# Sliding patterns

## Refresher

1  a  Find these pattern blocks.
      Rule a line, horizontally or vertically.
      Make a strip pattern.

   b  Look at these shapes. Decide how
      each shape is made. Rule a line, find
      the two tiles you need and place
      them on the line. Draw round the
      shape. Slide the shape in the
      direction of the arrow and re-draw
      several times. Colour the first two
      shapes in each pattern.

## Practice

1  Look at these shapes. Decide how
   these shapes were made. Make sliding
   patterns by translating each shape in
   the direction shown by the arrow.
   Colour the first two shapes in each
   pattern.

2  Find a way to make these overlap
   patterns. Copy and continue each
   pattern in three directions: horizontally
   … vertically … diagonally.
   Use colour to highlight part of each
   repetition.

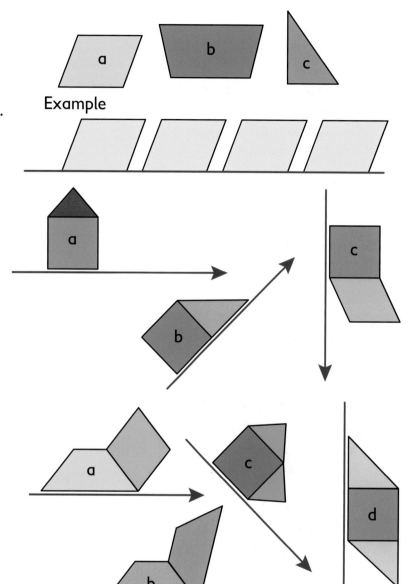

Example

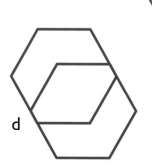

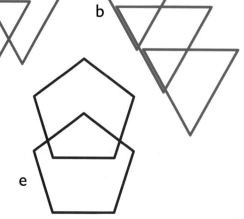

25

# Grid patterns

## Refresher

1 Choose one of these three patterns.
   Copy and continue it on squared paper.
   Remember, you can move in any direction.

2 Make a pattern of your own choice on the
   squared paper.

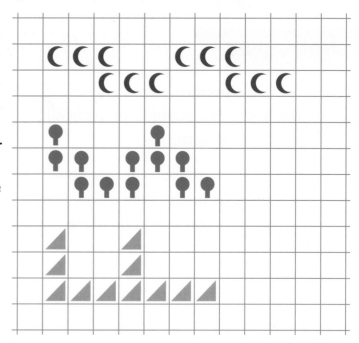

## Practice

1 Identify the motif in these patterns.
   Copy and continue each pattern on squared paper.
   Colour alternate motifs.

a
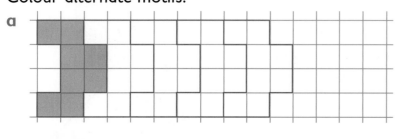

b
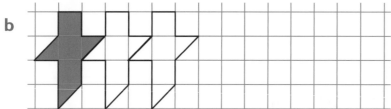

2 Do the same for these grid patterns. You need triangular paper.

a
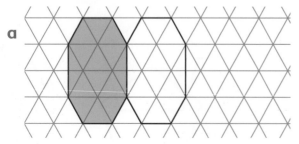

b
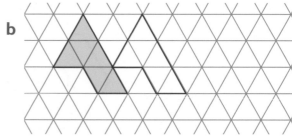

# Cut and slide patterns

## Refresher and Practice

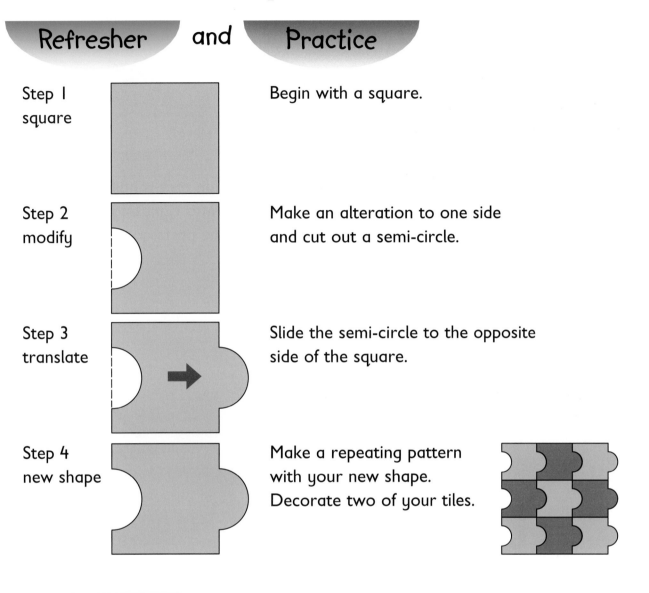

Step 1
square

Begin with a square.

Step 2
modify

Make an alteration to one side
and cut out a semi-circle.

Step 3
translate

Slide the semi-circle to the opposite
side of the square.

Step 4
new shape

Make a repeating pattern
with your new shape.
Decorate two of your tiles.

## Practice

Take another square. Follow the steps to make this tile.
Decorate it in an interesting way. Make a repeating pattern with your new shape.

Step 1        Step 2        Step 3        Step 4        Step 5

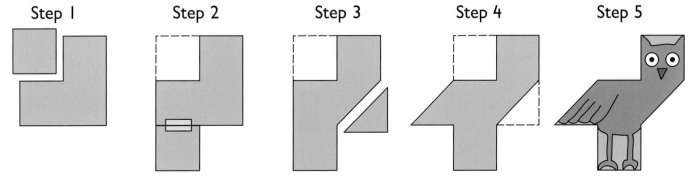

# Fancy angles

## Refresher

You need a 45°, 45°, 90° set square or half right angle measurer

1 a Draw a fan that is a quarter open.
   b Divide it into 45° parts.
   c Colour the parts blue and gold.

2 a Draw a fan that is half open.
   b Divide it into right angles.
   c Colour the parts gold and brown.

## Practice

1 How many half right angles do these fans show?
  Use a set square to help you.

a            b           c

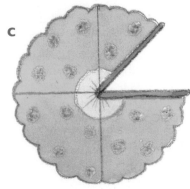

2 a Draw this fan shape.
   Colour 90° blue.
   Colour the 45° parts gold.
  b Find 2 more ways to colour the fan.

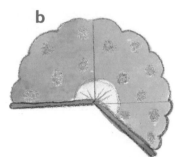

3 a Draw this fan shape.
   Colour 90° blue.
   Colour the 45° parts gold.
  b Find three more ways to colour the fan.
  c What if two parts are 90°.
   How many different ways can you colour the fan?

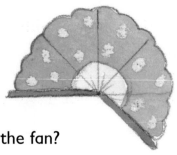

● Begin to know that angles are measured in degrees ...
● Solve mathematical shape problems or puzzles ...

Su 6, 2

# Getting in shape

## Refresher

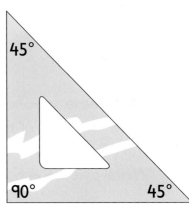

You need a 45°, 45°, 90° set square or half right angle measurer

1  Look at the shapes below. Write the letters of the shapes which have
   **a** four angles of 90°     **b** one angle of 90°

2  Write the letters of the shapes which have two angles of 45°.

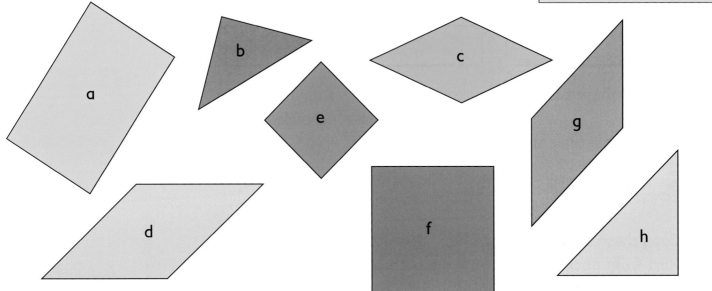

## Practice

1  You need 4 identical right-angled isosceles triangles.
   **a** Make this shape.
   **b**

> *You can make 10 different shapes using 4 identical right-angled triangles.*

   True or false? Investigate.
   Draw each shape you find.
   Remember: Shapes must be placed with equal side against equal side.

2  You need 12 straws which are the same length.
   Arrange them to make 4 squares.
   Make a careful drawing of what you did.
   Remember: Bending straws is not allowed.

# Pot luck

## Refresher

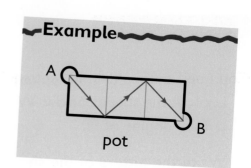

pot

1 Copy these snooker tables on to squared paper.
Draw the path of the ball which rolls at 45°.
Start from A each time.
Write **pot** if the ball drops into pocket B.

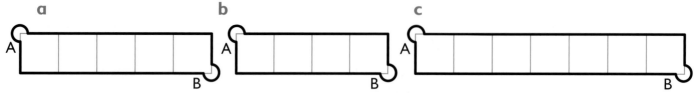

a      b      c

2 a Draw these tables: 1 square wide 10 squares long,
               1 square wide and 15 squares long.

   b Find out if they are pot or miss.

## Practice

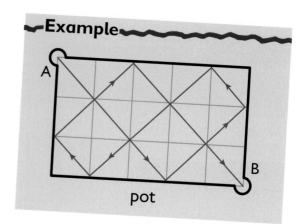

pot

1 Copy these snooker tables on to squared paper.
Start from pocket A and draw the path of the ball
which rolls and rebounds at 45° each time.
Write **pot** if the ball drops into pocket B.

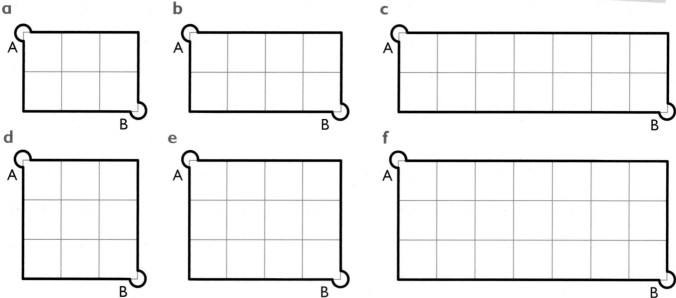

a      b      c

d      e      f

2 Draw 2 different two-pocket snooker tables where the ball will **pot** each time.

30

# Number sequences

## Refresher

Copy and complete the number lines by filling in the missing numbers.

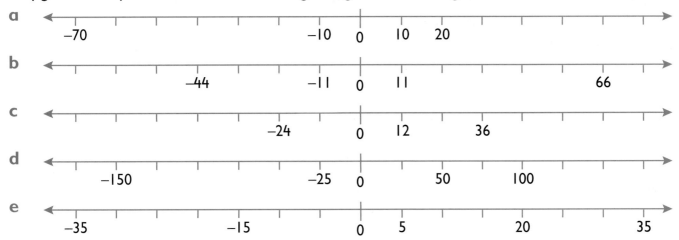

a
   −70                           −10  0   10   20

b
            −44         −11  0   11               66

c
                −24     0   12      36

d
    −150              −25  0       50     100

e
  −35           −15        0   5        20         35

## Practice

Look at the number sequences below.

Can you predict what numbers will come next?

Use your own hundred square to copy and continue each pattern.

Use a 101 to 200 square to keep the sequences going.

Can you see any patterns?

| 1 | 2 | 3 | 4 | 5 | 6 | 7 | 8 | 9 | 10 |
|---|---|---|---|---|---|---|---|---|---|
| 11 | 12 | 13 | 14 | 15 | 16 | 17 | 18 | 19 | 20 |
| 21 | 22 | 23 | 24 | 25 | 26 | 27 | 28 | 29 | 30 |
| 31 | 32 | 33 | 34 | 35 | 36 | 37 | 38 | 39 | 40 |
| 41 | 42 | 43 | 44 | 45 | 46 | 47 | 48 | 49 | 50 |
| 51 | 52 | 53 | 54 | 55 | 56 | 57 | 58 | 59 | 60 |
| 61 | 62 | 63 | 64 | 65 | 66 | 67 | 68 | 69 | 70 |
| 71 | 72 | 73 | 74 | 75 | 76 | 77 | 78 | 79 | 80 |
| 81 | 82 | 83 | 84 | 85 | 86 | 87 | 88 | 89 | 90 |
| 91 | 92 | 93 | 94 | 95 | 96 | 97 | 98 | 99 | 100 |

| 1 | 2 | 3 | 4 | 5 | 6 | 7 | 8 | 9 | 10 |
|---|---|---|---|---|---|---|---|---|---|
| 11 | 12 | 13 | 14 | 15 | 16 | 17 | 18 | 19 | 20 |
| 21 | 22 | 23 | 24 | 25 | 26 | 27 | 28 | 29 | 30 |
| 31 | 32 | 33 | 34 | 35 | 36 | 37 | 38 | 39 | 40 |
| 41 | 42 | 43 | 44 | 45 | 46 | 47 | 48 | 49 | 50 |
| 51 | 52 | 53 | 54 | 55 | 56 | 57 | 58 | 59 | 60 |
| 61 | 62 | 63 | 64 | 65 | 66 | 67 | 68 | 69 | 70 |
| 71 | 72 | 73 | 74 | 75 | 76 | 77 | 78 | 79 | 80 |
| 81 | 82 | 83 | 84 | 85 | 86 | 87 | 88 | 89 | 90 |
| 91 | 92 | 93 | 94 | 95 | 96 | 97 | 98 | 99 | 100 |

# Mixed multiples

## Refresher

Write the numbers that occur in each sequence in the correct order.

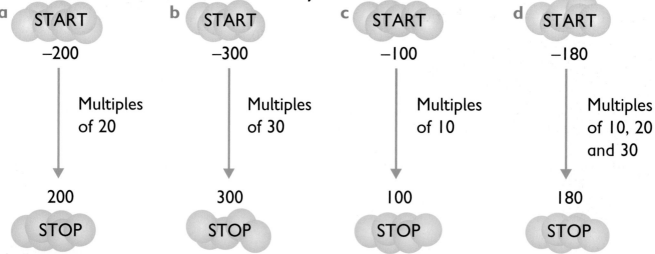

a  START
−200
Multiples of 20
↓
200
STOP

b  START
−300
Multiples of 30
↓
300
STOP

c  START
−100
Multiples of 10
↓
100
STOP

d  START
−180
Multiples of 10, 20 and 30
↓
180
STOP

## Practice

This underwater diver is searching for related fish.
Help him to find the multiples of 20 fish and the multiples of 30 fish.
Draw your own number lines and put the numbers in the correct order.

# Finding multiples

## Refresher

Inside the treasure chest, lots of numbers were found.
Sort them into multiples of 2, 3 and 4.

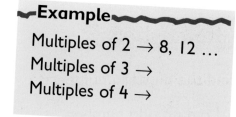

**Example**
Multiples of 2 → 8, 12 …
Multiples of 3 →
Multiples of 4 →

## Practice

Draw your own Venn Diagrams like the ones below.
Sort the numbers 1 to 40 to match the labels.
Write any numbers that belong in both sets in the middle.

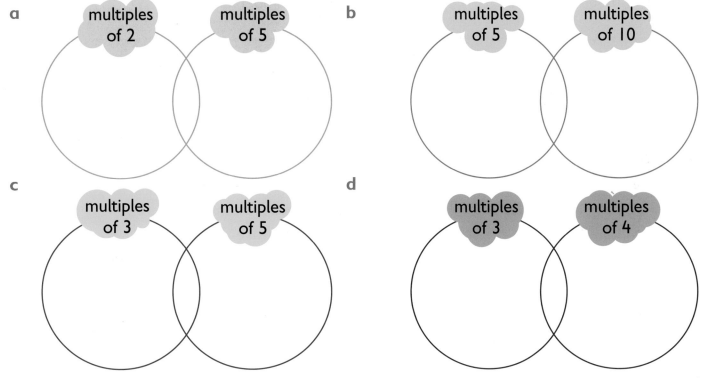

a  multiples of 2   multiples of 5

b  multiples of 5   multiples of 10

c  multiples of 3   multiples of 5

d  multiples of 3   multiples of 4

# Mystery numbers

## Refresher

Find the mystery numbers.

**a** I am an odd number.
I am between 20 and 25.
I am a multiple of 3.
What number am I?

**b** I am a multiple of 10.
I am between 100 and 200.
My digits add to make a total of 3.
What number am I?

**c** I am less than 20.
I am a multiple of 3 and 4.
What number am I?

**d** I am a multiple of 5.
I am an even number.
I am between 81 and 99.
What number am I?

## Practice

Try to find these mystery numbers.

**a** I think of a number.
I multiply by 3 and then add 4.
The answer is 16.
What number am I?

**b** I am an odd number.
I am a multiple of 3 and 5.
I am less than 30.
What number am I?

**c** I think of a number.
My double is half of 100.
What number am I?

**d** There are two of us.
We have 2 in the tens place.
We are not multiples of any numbers
except 1 and ourselves.
What numbers are we?

**e** I think of a number. Add 3.
Then multiply by 3.
The answer is 33.
What number am I?

**f** We are between 10 and 100.
Our digits are the same.
We are multiples of 11.
What are we?

# Missing numbers

## Refresher

Use the numbers 1 to 10 to make these statements correct. For each number sentence a different shape indicates a different number.

a

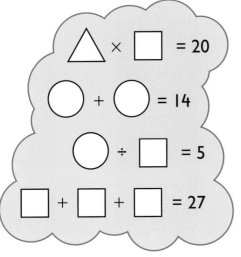

b

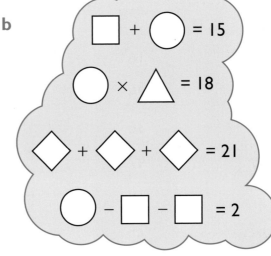

## Practice

Replace the circles with the digits ⏹1 ⏹4 ⏹5 ⏹9 to make each statement true.

1

**LOST AND FOUND**

a ◯◯ – ◯ = 36

b ◯◯ + ◯ = 63

c ◯◯ + ◯◯ = 100

d ◯◯ × ◯ = 70

e ◯◯ – ◯◯ = 54

f ◯◯◯ + ◯ = 460

g ◯◯ × ◯ = 49

2

**LOST AND FOUND**

a ◯◯ ÷ ◯ = 5

b ◯◯ + ◯◯ = 136

c ◯◯ × ◯ = 135

d ◯◯ – ◯◯ = 46

e ◯◯ + ◯◯ = 64

f ◯◯ × ◯ = 205

g ◯◯◯ – ◯ = 486

35

# Finding remainders

## Refresher

Play "Find the multiple".
Look at the numbers below. Write the multiple that is closest to, but not over, each number.

| a 2 | b 5 | c 3 | d 10 | e 4 |
|---|---|---|---|---|
| 13 | 16 | 23 | 15 | 14 |
| 25 | 24 | 16 | 27 | 9 |
| 17 | 36 | 7 | 36 | 30 |
| 11 | 47 | 32 | 49 | 22 |
| 29 | 18 | 25 | 83 | 19 |
| 14 | 29 | 14 | 75 | 37 |

## Practice

1 Look at each division problem.
Write the multiplication fact you think of to answer the problem.
Write the answer to the problem and any remainders.

a 36 ÷ 5
27 ÷ 4
52 ÷ 10
17 ÷ 3
25 ÷ 6

7 × 5 = 35
36 ÷ 5 = 7 r 1

b 43 ÷ 4
23 ÷ 2
27 ÷ 8
39 ÷ 6
26 ÷ 3

c 35 ÷ 4
53 ÷ 5
29 ÷ 3
74 ÷ 10
15 ÷ 2

2 Find the missing number to make each calculation correct.

32 = (6 × 5) + ☐

46 = (7 × 6) + ☐

56 = (5 × 10) + ☐

26 = (8 × 3) + ☐

19 = (4 × 4) + ☐

49 = (9 × 5) + ☐

436 = (4 × 100) + ☐

78 = (7 × 10) + ☐

367 = (3 × 100) + ☐

77 = (9 × 8) + ☐

# Rounding remainders ☆

## Refresher

Find the answer to these division problems.
Be careful, some have remainders.

**a**
24 ÷ 4 = ☐

33 ÷ 3 = ☐

27 ÷ 5 = ☐

18 ÷ 2 = ☐

15 ÷ 4 = ☐

**b**
29 ÷ 4 = ☐

36 ÷ 6 = ☐

23 ÷ 3 = ☐

85 ÷ 10 = ☐

90 ÷ 10 = ☐

**c**
16 ÷ 4 = ☐

22 ÷ 5 = ☐

19 ÷ 3 = ☐

34 ÷ 4 = ☐

47 ÷ 5 = ☐

## Practice

Read each story. Write the division fact and the answer.
If there is a remainder, think carefully whether you need
to round your answer up or down.

**a** 27 people are going to the moon. Each rocket can take a maximum of 4 people. How many rockets are needed?

**b** There are 38 spacesuits. Each rocket has enough space for 5 spacesuits. How many rockets carry a total of 5 spacesuits?

**c** There are 34 helmets. Each astronaut needs 4 helmets. How many astronauts can travel into space?

**d** There are 52 weeks in a year. A rocket is launched every 10 weeks. How many launches in a year?

**e** 24 satellites are to be sent into space. 5 satellites can be sent a month. How many months until they are all up in space?

**f** Photographs of the rocket cost £6 each. I have £34. How many photographs can I buy?

# More about the 9 times table

## Refresher

The answers to the 9 times table are locked away in the treasure chest. Search this page for the "key facts" and use them to help you work out the answers.

**a**
1 × 9 = ☐
5 × 9 = ☐
10 × 9 = ☐
2 × 9 = ☐

**b**
3 × 9 = ☐
0 × 9 = ☐
8 × 9 = ☐
6 × 9 = ☐

**c**
9 × 9 = ☐
4 × 9 = ☐
7 × 9 = ☐
11 × 9 = ☐

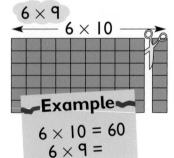

**d**
☐ × 9 = 27
☐ × 9 = 54
☐ × 9 = 45
☐ × 9 = 81

**e**
9 × ☐ = 90
9 × ☐ = 36
9 × ☐ = 9
9 × ☐ = 18

**f**
9 × ☐ = 0
☐ × 3 = 27
☐ × 9 = 63
9 × ☐ = 72

## Practice

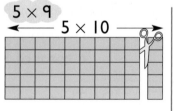

Use the 10 times table to help you work out the answers to the 9 times table.

6 × 9
◄── 6 × 10 ──►
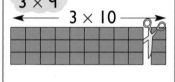
**Example**
6 × 10 = 60
6 × 9 =

3 × 9
◄── 3 × 10 ──►

5 × 9
◄── 5 × 10 ──►

9 × 9
◄── 9 × 10 ──►
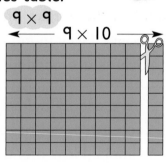

10 × 9
◄── 10 × 10 ──►
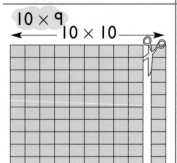

6 × 9
◄── 6 × 10 ──►
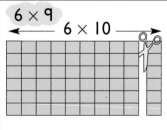

4 × 9
◄── 4 × 10 ──►
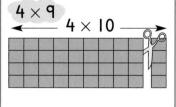

7 × 9
◄── 7 × 10 ──►
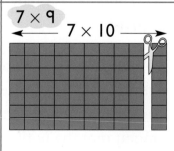

38

# Finding out about sevens

## Refresher

$2 \times 7 = 14$

The answers to the 7 times table are locked away in the treasure chest. Search this page for the "key facts" and use them to help you work out the answers.

a
$2 \times 7 =$ ☐
$5 \times 7 =$ ☐
$1 \times 7 =$ ☐
$10 \times 7 =$ ☐

b
$0 \times 7 =$ ☐
$4 \times 7 =$ ☐
$9 \times 7 =$ ☐
$7 \times 7 =$ ☐

c
$3 \times 7 =$ ☐
$6 \times 7 =$ ☐
$11 \times 7 =$ ☐
$8 \times 7 =$ ☐

$5 \times 7 = 35$

$10 \times 7 = 70$

d
$7 \times$ ☐ $= 35$
$7 \times$ ☐ $= 7$
$7 \times$ ☐ $= 56$
$7 \times$ ☐ $= 21$

e
☐ $\times 7 = 28$
☐ $\times 7 = 63$
☐ $\times 7 = 49$
☐ $\times 7 = 77$

f
☐ $\times 7 = 70$
$7 \times$ ☐ $= 14$
$7 \times$ ☐ $= 0$
☐ $\times 7 = 42$

## Practice

$1 \times 7 = 7$

Multiply the numbers on the first card. Turn over the card and multiply the numbers again. What do you notice?

$7 \times 3$ → $3 \times 7$

$7 \times 5$ → $5 \times 7$

$7 \times 10$ → $10 \times 7$

$7 \times 4$ → $4 \times 7$

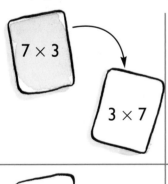
$7 \times 6$ → $6 \times 7$

$7 \times 9$ → $9 \times 7$

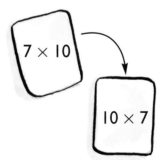
$7 \times 8$ → $8 \times 7$

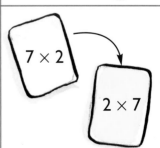
$7 \times 2$ → $2 \times 7$

# Multiplying larger numbers

## Refresher

Partition each of these calculations to find the answer.

**Example**
$32 \times 3 = (30 \times 3) + (2 \times 3)$
$= 90 + 6$
$= 96$

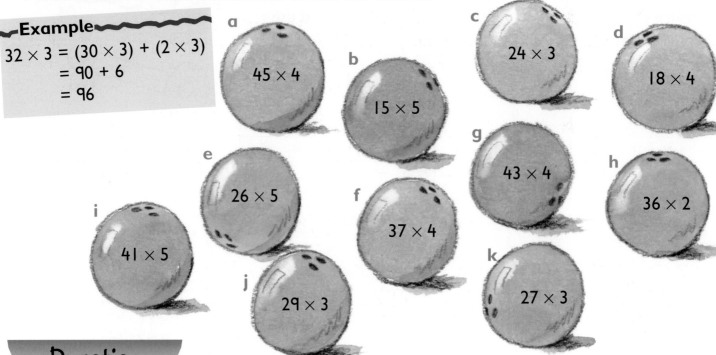

a $45 \times 4$

b $15 \times 5$

c $24 \times 3$

d $18 \times 4$

e $26 \times 5$

f $37 \times 4$

g $43 \times 4$

h $36 \times 2$

i $41 \times 5$

j $29 \times 3$

k $27 \times 3$

## Practice

1  Knock down the bowling pins using a ball of your choice.
   Multiply the number on the ball by the number on the
   bowling pin to get your score. Have 10 goes.

26  63  16  62

43  35  37  54

24  45  18  14  29

3  5  6  4  9

2  What was your highest score? Write the calculation.
3  What was your lowest score? Write the calculation.

# Raising money

## Refresher

Read each problem. Decide whether you will use × or ÷. Approximate the answer.

**a** 4 children collected £5·37 each. How much altogether?

| × or ÷ | Approx: |

**b** Maria raised £37 for reading 4 books. How much did she raise per book?

| × or ÷ | Approx: |

**c** John's parents gave him a contribution of £3·30 each day of the school week. How much did he raise?

| × or ÷ | Approx: |

**d** A total of £98 was being sent to help 10 different children. How much will they each receive?

| × or ÷ | Approx: |

**e** Three countries will be given £57 each. How much altogether?

| × or ÷ | Approx: |

## Practice

Read each problem. Find the important information.
Write a calculation for each problem.
Give your answer in £.p where necessary.

**a** Joshua raised £23 for reading 5 books. How much did he raise per book?

**b** Year 4 had a skipathon to raise money. They made £61 for 2 hours of skipping. How much did they make per hour?

**c** Year 5 raised £64 from their sponsored silence. The silence lasted 10 minutes. How much did they raise per minute?

**d** Year 4 children raised £47 to send to 5 children in need. How much will each child receive?

**e** Tina saved up her pocket money for 4 weeks. She gave £13 to charity. How much money does she get per week?

**f** £43 was raised in Year 3 over a 4-week period. How much did they raise per week?

# Doubling and halving multiples of 100

## Refresher

1  Double each number.

a 27
b 44
c 33
d 18
e 39

2  Halve each number.

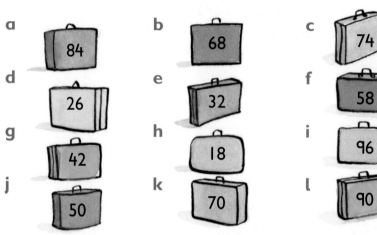

a 84
b 68
c 74
d 26
e 32
f 58
g 42
h 18
i 96
j 50
k 70
l 90

## Practice

1  Find the multiples of 100. Double them.
   Record your answer in 2 different ways.

**Example**
400 + 400 = 800
400 × 2 = 800

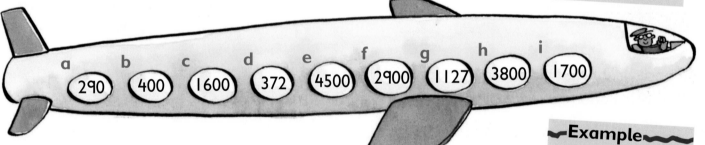

a 290  b 400  c 1600  d 372  e 4500  f 2900  g 1127  h 3800  i 1700

2  Find the multiples of 100. Halve them.
   Record your answer in 2 different ways.

**Example**
8200 ÷ 2 = 4100
$\frac{1}{2}$ × 8200 = 4100

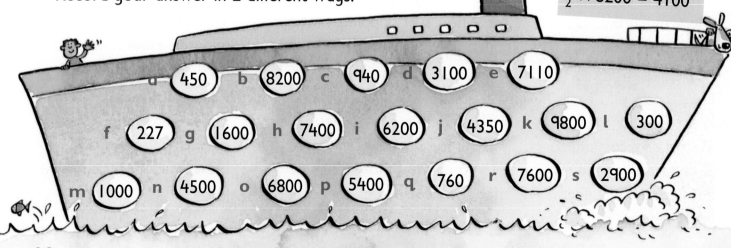

a 450  b 8200  c 940  d 3100  e 7110
f 227  g 1600  h 7400  i 6200  j 4350  k 9800  l 300
m 1000  n 4500  o 6800  p 5400  q 760  r 7600  s 2900

# Multiplication and division Lucky Dip

## Refresher

Some of these calculations are incorrect.
Find the incorrect calculations.
Write the calculation and the correct answer.

$2 \times 75 = 145$

$5 \times 60 = 30$

$10 \times 52 = 5200$

$3 \times 40 = 340$

$4 \times 35 = 120$

$10 \times 68 = 78$

$4 \times 40 = 160$

$10 \times 74 = 740$

$3 \times 27 = 327$

$2 \times 45 = 90$

$4 \times 46 = 184$

$3 \times 52 = 150$

$5 \times 30 = 150$

## Practice

**Example**

$352 \times 10 = 3520$

Complete each calculation in the boxes.

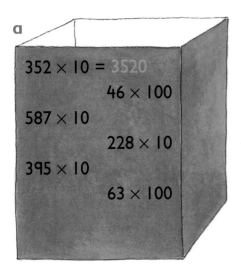

**a**

$352 \times 10 = 3520$

$46 \times 100$

$587 \times 10$

$228 \times 10$

$395 \times 10$

$63 \times 100$

**b**

$2000 \div 100$

$8000 \div 10$

$7000 \div 10$

$4000 \div 100$

$3000 \div 10$

$6000 \div 100$

$1000 \div 100$

$9000 \div 10$

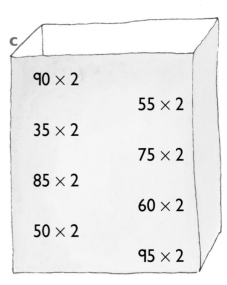

**c**

$90 \times 2$

$55 \times 2$

$35 \times 2$

$75 \times 2$

$85 \times 2$

$60 \times 2$

$50 \times 2$

$95 \times 2$

# Recording division

## Refresher

Approximate the answer to each calculation.

a  36 ÷ 3 = ☐        f  64 ÷ 2 = ☐        k  76 ÷ 4 = ☐

b  48 ÷ 4 = ☐        g  82 ÷ 2 = ☐        l  57 ÷ 3 = ☐

c  55 ÷ 5 = ☐        h  93 ÷ 3 = ☐        m 76 ÷ 2 = ☐

d  84 ÷ 4 = ☐        i  69 ÷ 3 = ☐        n  84 ÷ 3 = ☐

e  39 ÷ 3 = ☐        j  46 ÷ 2 = ☐        o  96 ÷ 4 = ☐

## Practice

Aeroplane seats are arranged in rows of 2, 3, 4 or 5.
Find out how many rows of each were filled.
Approximate your answer first. Record your
work using the standard method of division.

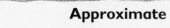

**Approximate**

78 ÷ 3 → (80 ÷ 4 = 20)

```
    3 ) 78
       -30    (10×3)
        48
       -30    (10×3)
        18
       -18    (6×3)
         0
```

Answer = 26

**Approximate**

78 ÷ 3 → (75 ÷ 3 = 25)

```
    3 ) 78
       -60    (20×3)
        18
       -18    (6×3)
         0
```

Answer = 26

**1**

a  72 seats        b   56 seats
c  94 seats        d   38 seats

**2**

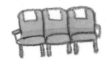 

a  78 seats        b   48 seats
c  51 seats        d   87 seats

**3**

a  92 seats        b   76 seats
c  52 seats        d   68 seats

**4**

a  65 seats        b   90 seats
c  75 seats        d   85 seats

# Problems on safari

## Refresher

The question for each of the problems below is missing.
Read the problems carefully and write a question to match.

| | |
|---|---|
| **a** Mr and Mrs Wallis hired a jeep for 1 week. The cost of the jeep for 1 day was £24. | **b** 4 groups of lions were seen altogether on safari. Each pride had 9 lions. |
| **c** The Wallises bought 2 pairs of binoculars for £54. | **d** Each day, for 2 weeks, Mr and Mrs Wallis used 3 rolls of film photographing the animals. |
| **e** 16 zebras, 2 lions, 12 hippos and 35 elephants were seen on Monday. | **f** The Wallises visited in the middle of summer. The hottest day had temperatures of 36°C. The coolest day recorded a temperature of 30°C. |

## Practice

Read the story problems.
Choose an appropriate method of calculating your answer.
● mental ● mental with jottings ● paper and pencil (standard method).

| | |
|---|---|
| **a** Mr and Mrs Merton went on safari to Kenya. The total cost of travel insurance was £120 for 12 days. How much did it cost per day? | **b** The cost of hiring a jeep is £48 for 3 days or £98 for 7 days. Which deal costs less, per day? |
| **c** Over 3 days, Mr and Mrs Merton saw 27 rhinos. If they saw the same number each time, how many did they see each day? | **d** The hotel room cost £36 a day for the first 5 days and £27 for each day after that. How much does it cost to stay at the hotel for 8 days? |
| **e** The Mertons hired a local guide and a driver for 7 days. The guide cost £7 a day and the driver £9 a day. What was their total bill? | **f** Mr Merton bought 2 films for each day of the 12 day holiday. Films cost £4 each. How much did he spend on films? |

45

# Assorted biscuit problems

## Refresher

1 A biscuit has 3 cherries.
  a How many cherries on 2 biscuits?
  b If there are 9 cherries, how many biscuits are there?

2 Copy and complete the table.

| Biscuits | 1 | 2 | 3 | 4 | 5 | 6 | 10 |
|----------|---|---|---|---|---|---|----|
| Cherries |   |   |   |   |   |   |    |

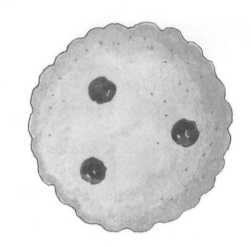

## Practice

1 Copy and complete the tables.

a

Buy 5 packets get this free gift

| Packets    | 5 | 10 | 20 |   |   | 50 |
|------------|---|----|----|---|---|----|
| Free gifts | 1 |    |    | 6 | 7 |    |

b

Buy 2 packets   Get 1 free

| Packets bought | 2 |   | 8 |   | 20 |    |
|----------------|---|---|---|---|----|----|
| Free packets   |   | 2 |   | 6 |    | 15 |

c

Buy 4 cakes get 1 free

| Number of cakes | 4 |   | 16 |   |   | 36 |
|-----------------|---|---|----|---|---|----|
| Free cakes      |   | 3 |    | 6 | 8 |    |

2 How many biscuit men can
  you make using these shapes?

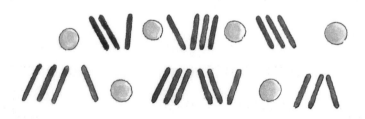

# Broken parts

## Refresher

1 Copy and complete the sentences.

a [ 1 ] out of [ 4 ] eggs are cracked.

b [ ] out of [ ] eggs are cracked.

c [ ] out of [ ] eggs are cracked.

d [ ] out of [ ] eggs are cracked.

2 Copy and continue each pattern.
Then copy and complete the sentences.

a  1 in every [ ] eggs are cracked.

b  1 in every [ ] eggs are cracked.

c 1 in every [ ] eggs are cracked.

d 2 in every [ ] eggs are cracked.

## Practice

1 Copy and complete the sentences.

a  [ ] in 4 are broken.

[ ] in 8 are broken.

5 in [ ] are broken.

b 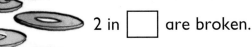 1 in [ ] are broken.

2 in [ ] are broken.

[ ] in 15 are broken.

c 1 in [ 5 ] plates are broken.

2 in [ ] plates are broken.

3 in [ ] plates are broken.

5 in [ ] plates are broken.

[ ] in 50 plates are broken.

d 1 in [ ] plates are broken.

2 in [ 12 ] plates are broken.

[ ] in 18 plates are broken.

6 in [ ] plates are broken.

[ ] in 60 plates are broken.

# Fractions and decimals

## Refresher

1 Write the missing decimals and fractions.

**Example**

a $\frac{3}{10} = 0\cdot3$

b $\frac{7}{10} = \boxed{\phantom{x}}$

c $\boxed{\phantom{x}} = 0\cdot9$

d $\boxed{\phantom{x}} = 0\cdot1$

e $\frac{1}{2} = \boxed{\phantom{x}}$

f $\boxed{\phantom{x}} = 0\cdot2$

2 Write the missing decimals and fractions.

a $2\frac{3}{10} = \boxed{\phantom{x}}$

b $1\frac{8}{10} = \boxed{\phantom{x}}$

c $\boxed{\phantom{x}} = 4\cdot5$

d $\boxed{\phantom{x}} = 9\cdot2$

e $5\frac{1}{10} = \boxed{\phantom{x}}$

f $\boxed{\phantom{x}} = 15\cdot4$

## Practice

1 Write these amounts using pounds and pence.

a 70p = £0·70

b 40p = £$\boxed{\phantom{x}}$

c $\frac{1}{2}$ of £1 = £$\boxed{\phantom{x}}$

d 6p = £$\boxed{\phantom{x}}$

e $\frac{9}{10}$ of £1 = £$\boxed{\phantom{x}}$

f 10p = £$\boxed{\phantom{x}}$

2 Copy and fill in the missing amounts.

a £3·50 = 350p

b £1·26 = $\boxed{\phantom{x}}$

c £2·90 = $\boxed{\phantom{x}}$

d £4·05 = $\boxed{\phantom{x}}$

e £$\boxed{\phantom{x}}$ = 423p

f £$\boxed{\phantom{x}}$ = 750p

g £$\boxed{\phantom{x}}$ = 210p

3 Change these lengths to centimetres.

a 0·7 cm = 70 cm

b $\frac{3}{10}$ m = $\boxed{\phantom{x}}$

c 0·4 m = $\boxed{\phantom{x}}$

d 0·48 m = $\boxed{\phantom{x}}$

e $\frac{1}{2}$ m = $\boxed{\phantom{x}}$

f 2·2 m = $\boxed{\phantom{x}}$

g $1\frac{9}{10}$ m = $\boxed{\phantom{x}}$

4 Change these lengths to metres.

a 30 cm = $\boxed{\phantom{x}}$ m

b 112 cm = $\boxed{\phantom{x}}$ m

c 450 cm = $\boxed{\phantom{x}}$ m

d 203 cm = $\boxed{\phantom{x}}$ m

# Machine maths

## Refresher

**1** Copy and complete the table.

| decimal fraction | 0·1 | | 0·25 | | 0·4 | | 0·6 | | 0·75 | | 0·9 |
|---|---|---|---|---|---|---|---|---|---|---|---|
| fraction | | $\frac{2}{10}$ | | $\frac{3}{10}$ | | $\frac{1}{2}$ | | $\frac{7}{10}$ | | $\frac{8}{10}$ | |

**2** Write the missing decimals and fractions.

**a** $2\frac{3}{10} = 2·3$    **b** $1\frac{1}{2} = \Box$    **c** $5\frac{1}{4} = \Box$    **d** $\Box = 3·9$

**e** $\Box = 6·5$    **f** $\Box = 1·75$    **g** $1\frac{1}{10} = \Box$    **h** $9\frac{3}{4} = \Box$

**3** Change the times to minutes.

**a** $\frac{2}{10}$ hour   12 minutes    **b** $\frac{1}{2}$ hour    **c** $\frac{1}{4}$ hour

**d** $\frac{1}{10}$ hour    **e** $\frac{3}{4}$ hour    **f** $\frac{3}{10}$ hour

## Practice

**1** Write these amounts using pounds and pence.

**a** $\frac{6}{10}$ of £1   £0·60    **b** $\frac{2}{10}$ of £1    **c** $\frac{3}{4}$ of £1

**d** $\frac{1}{2}$ of £1    **e** $\frac{1}{4}$ of £1    **f** $\frac{7}{10}$ of £1

**2** Write these amounts as fractions of £1.

**a** 20p   $\frac{2}{10}$ of £1    **b** 25p    **c** 90p

**d** 75p    **e** 10p    **f** 50p

**3** Change these lengths to centimetres.

**a** 0·7 m    **b** 0·25 m    **c** $\frac{1}{2}$ m

**d** 2·2 m    **e** $1\frac{3}{4}$ m    **f** 4·9 m

**4** Change these times to minutes.

**a** 0·5 hour    **b** 0·1 hour    **c** 0·25 hour    **d** 0·75 hour

**5** Write these in order, smallest to largest.

**a** $\frac{7}{10}$ of £1, £0·65, 60p, $\frac{3}{4}$ of £1    **b** $\frac{3}{10}$ m, 0·2 m, $\frac{1}{4}$ m, 0·28 m

**c** 1·3 m, 120 cm, $1\frac{1}{4}$ m, $1\frac{4}{10}$ m    **d** 435 cm, 4·2 m, $4\frac{3}{4}$ m, 4·60 m

**49**

# Counter fractions and decimals

## Refresher

Describe the number of blue counters three ways if possible.

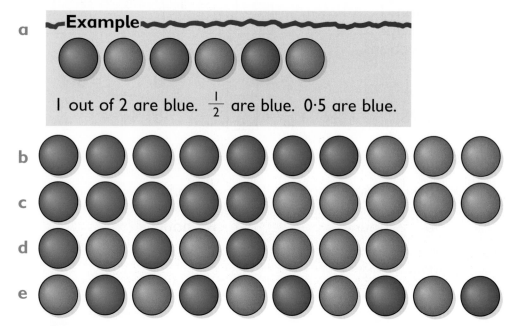

a **Example**

1 out of 2 are blue.  $\frac{1}{2}$  are blue.  0·5 are blue.

b

c

d

e

## Practice

Work in pairs. You will need: a bag, red and blue counters

1  One person takes 10 counters
   from a bag.
   The other person describes
   the blue counters.
   Do this twice each.

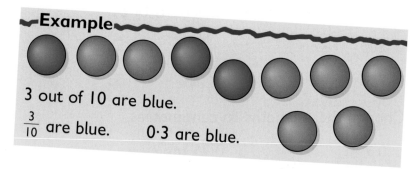

**Example**

3 out of 10 are blue.

$\frac{3}{10}$ are blue.        0·3 are blue.

2  Take turns to take 4 counters from the bag.
   Describe the blue counters. Do this twice each.

3  Take turns to take 5 counters from the bag.
   Describe the blue counters. Do this twice each.

50

# Adding and subtracting

## Refresher

1 Make 5 addition and 5 subtraction calculations choosing two numbers each time.

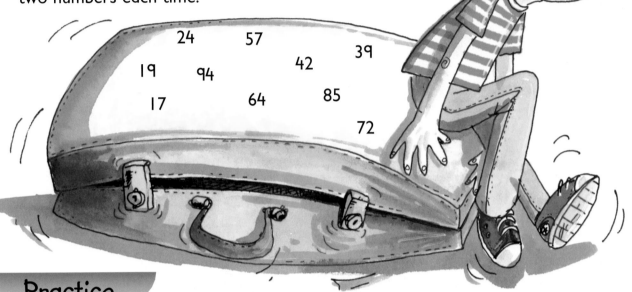

24    57    39
19    94    42
17    64    85
72

## Practice

1 Choose three numbers each time to make 10 addition calculations. Work out each in reverse order to check your answer.

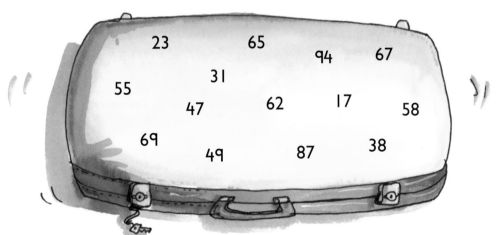

23    65    94    67
31    55
47    62    17    58
69    49    87    38

2 Work out these subtraction calculations. Work out the calculation in the brackets first.

a  (64 − 21) − 13
   64 − (21 − 13)

b  (68 − 26) − 14
   68 − (26 − 14)

c  (71 − 38) − 11
   71 − (38 − 11)

d  (94 − 52) − 16
   94 − (52 − 16)

e  (87 − 35) − 23
   87 − (35 − 23)

# Column addition

## Refresher

Write out the calculations vertically and work out the answer.

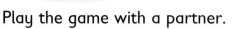

a
```
  1 3 6
+ 2 4 6
-------
  3 8 2
```

b  251 + 375
c  382 + 463
d  295 + 376
e  486 + 245
f  572 + 239
g  £4·68 + £2·16
h  £3·72 + £3·84
i  £7·65 + £2·87
j  £6·49 + £1·73

## Practice

Play the game with a partner.

You will need: a 1–6 die, 2 counters and pencil and paper

● Put your counters on start.
● Throw the die and move your counter.
● When you land on a calculation, work out the answer using the written method.

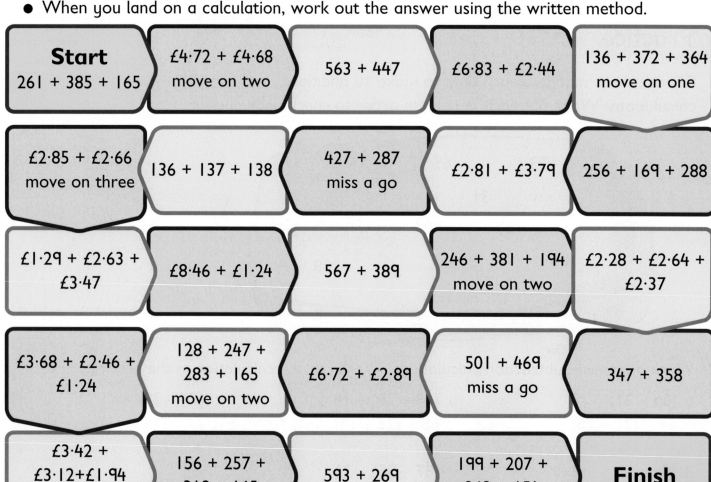

**Start** 261 + 385 + 165

£4·72 + £4·68 move on two

563 + 447

£6·83 + £2·44

136 + 372 + 364 move on one

£2·85 + £2·66 move on three

136 + 137 + 138

427 + 287 miss a go

£2·81 + £3·79

256 + 169 + 288

£1·29 + £2·63 + £3·47

£8·46 + £1·24

567 + 389

246 + 381 + 194 move on two

£2·28 + £2·64 + £2·37

£3·68 + £2·46 + £1·24

128 + 247 + 283 + 165 move on two

£6·72 + £2·89

501 + 469 miss a go

347 + 358

£3·42 + £3·12 + £1·94 miss a go

156 + 257 + 318 + 165

593 + 269

199 + 207 + 263 + 154

**Finish**

52

# Column subtraction

## Refresher

Write these calculations out vertically and then work out the answer.

a  342 – 137          b  451 – 236
c  563 – 281          d  675 – 381
e  472 – 135          f  513 – 267
g  603 – 347          h  £6·38 – £2·54
i  £5·31 – £2·65     j  £4·62 – £1·78

~Example~

$$\begin{array}{r} 6\ 3\ 8 \\ -2\ 4\ 9 \\ \hline \end{array}$$

## Practice

Play the game with a partner.
You will need: a 1–6 die, 2 counters and pencil and paper

● Put your counters on start.
● Throw the die and move your counter.
● When you land on a circle, work out the
  answer using the written method.

**Start**

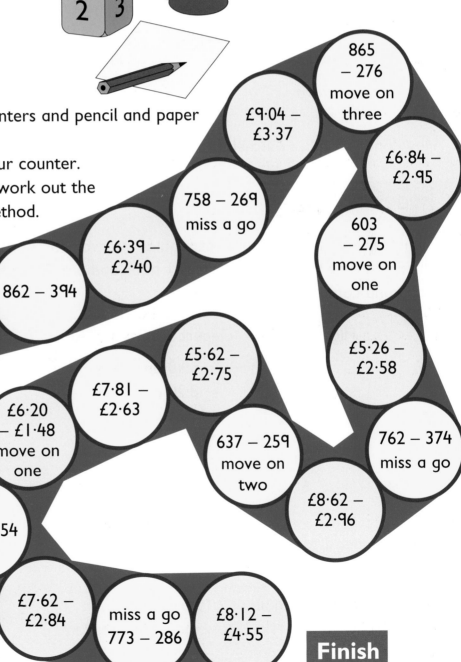

641 – 353

£2·64 – £1·85 move on two

862 – 394

£6·39 – £2·40

758 – 269 miss a go

£9·04 – £3·37

865 – 276 move on three

£6·84 – £2·95

603 – 275 move on one

£5·26 – £2·58

762 – 374 miss a go

£8·62 – £2·96

637 – 259 move on two

£5·62 – £2·75

£7·81 – £2·63

£6·20 – £1·48 move on one

831 – 354

£7·62 – £2·84

miss a go 773 – 286

£8·12 – £4·55

**Finish**

# Travelling times

## Refresher and Practice

1 A bus leaves Market Street Bus Station in the town for these villages.
The bus takes 10 minutes between each village stop.
Copy and complete the bus timetable.

| Market Street | 10:15 | | |
|---|---|---|---|
| Winterby | | | 12:45 |
| Clarkham | | | |
| Langton | | 11:05 | |
| Exford | | | |

2 How long is the bus journey from Market Street to the village of Exford?

## Practice

1 Flights leave Stansted Airport at regular intervals for Amsterdam.
The flying time between airports is 1 hour and 5 minutes.
Copy and complete the timetable.

| Flight number | Depart Stansted | Arrive Amsterdam |
|---|---|---|
| 1 | 6:40 am | |
| 2 | 8:20 am | |
| 3 | 11:25 am | |
| 4 | 2:00 pm | |
| 5 | 5:55 pm | |
| 6 | 8:30 pm | |

2 Flight number 2 takes off 35 minutes late.
At what time does it arrive in Amsterdam?

3 You arrive in Amsterdam at 7:15 p.m.
Which flight did you take? How many minutes late
did it arrive in Amsterdam?

54

# Calendar counting

## Refresher

1 a Copy this year's calendar for the month of February.
  b Circle the days when the Fontana Museum is open.

2 On which days throughout the year is the museum open?

3 On which day is it closed every month of the year?

4 For how many months is the museum open on Thursdays?

5 In which months is it closed on a Wednesday?

Fontana Museum
Opening Hours

Winter:
October – March
Saturday & Sunday
only

Summer:
April – September
daily, except Tuesdays

## Practice

1 Make a copy of this year's calendar for the month of September.

2 Your class is planning to visit the Fontana Museum in September.
  a Cross out the dates when the museum is closed.
  b Cross out the dates when your school is closed.
  c Your class visit will be in the third week of September.
    On which days might the visit be?
  Write the day and date for each.

3 Write the leap years between 1980 and 2008.

4 Use a calendar which is not a leap year.
  Write the dates for these days in the year:
  a 50th day    b 100th day    c 200th day.

5 On your calendar for the month of September, draw a
  rectangle round 9 dates to make three rows of three dates.
  a Add 8 to the smallest number in the rectangle,
    then multiply the answer by 9.
  b Total all 9 numbers.
  c Compare your answer for a and b.
    Write what you notice.
  d Repeat the above steps for other rectangles of 9 numbers.
    Does it always work? Explain.

SEPTEMBER

| | | | | |
|---|---|---|---|---|
| S | | 3 | 10 | 17 | 24 |
| M | | 4 | 11 | 18 | 25 |
| Tu | | 5 | 12 | 19 | 26 |
| W | | 6 | 13 | 20 | 27 |
| Th | | 7 | 14 | 21 | 28 |
| F | 1 | 8 | 15 | 22 | 29 |
| S | 2 | 9 | 16 | 23 | 30 |

# Shape Venn diagrams

## Refresher

1 Copy the Venn diagram.

2 Draw each shape in the correct place.

3 Count the shapes.
Write the numbers in the squares.

4 a How many squares are there?
b How many squares and triangles are there?
c How many shapes are not squares?
d How many shapes are not squares or triangles?
e How many shapes are there altogether?

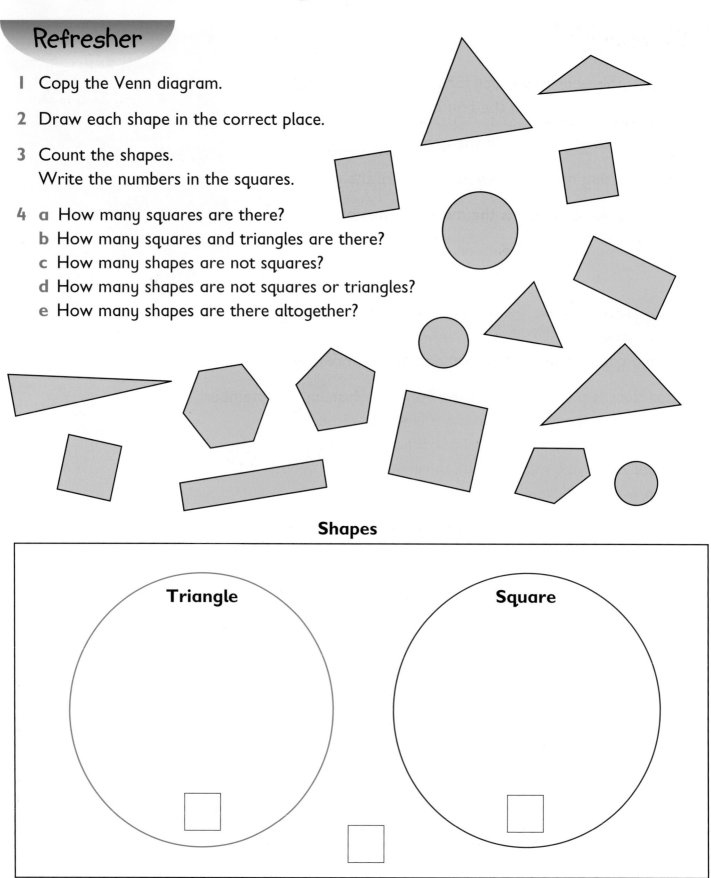

**Shapes**

Triangle          Square

## Practice

1 Copy the Venn diagram.

2 Draw each shape in the correct place.

3 Count the shapes.
Write the numbers in the squares.

4 a How many blue shapes are there?
b How many rectangles are there?
c How many blue rectangles are there?
d How many shapes are not blue?
e How many shapes are not blue rectangles?
f How many rectangles are not blue?
g Describe the shapes outside the sets.

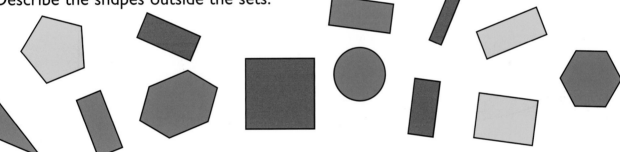

**Sorting coloured shapes**

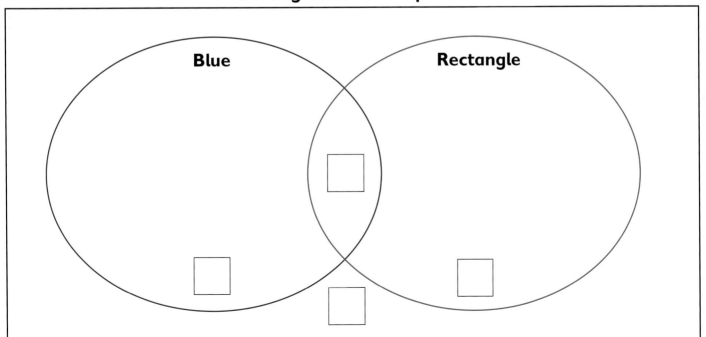

# Number Venn diagrams

## Refresher

1 Copy the Venn diagram.
   Write the numbers on your diagram.

2 Count the numbers.
   Write the totals in the squares.

3 a How many numbers are less than 20?
   b How many numbers are greater than 200?
   c How many numbers are in between 20 and 200?
   d How many numbers are not less than 20?
   e How many numbers are there altogether?

17
98
2  29     320
      1000
141        412
      135  16
              1
752   72   201

### Sorting numbers

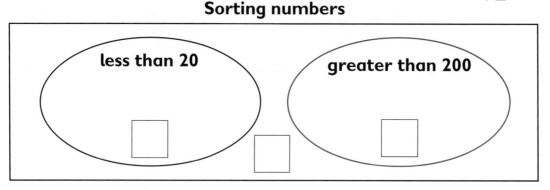

less than 20     greater than 200

4 Copy the Venn diagram below.
   Write the numbers on your diagram.

5 Count the numbers.
   Write the totals in the squares.

6 a How many two-digit numbers are there?
   b How many three-digit numbers are there?
   c How many numbers do not have two digits?
   d How many numbers do not have two or three digits?

231  52    9321
7            500
   5   2000  160
      99   999
              561
   4051  10
              100
              17
              9

### Sorting numbers

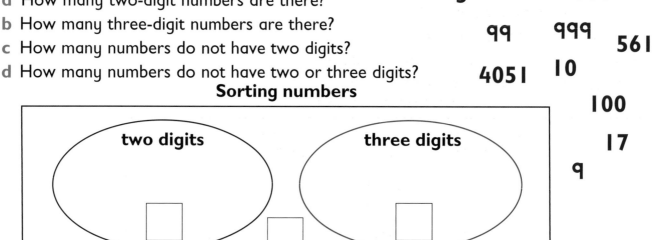

two digits     three digits

58

## Practice

1 Copy the Venn diagram.
Write the numbers on your diagram.

2 Count the numbers.
Write the totals in the squares.

3 a How many numbers are less than 50?
  b How many even numbers are less than 50?
  c How many numbers are not even?
  d How many even numbers are not less than 50?
  e How many numbers are not even and not less than 50?
  f Describe the numbers in the intersection.

37    100    3

42  52  305

6  1024  33

71  255

64

18  38  9

83

136

47

**Sorting numbers**

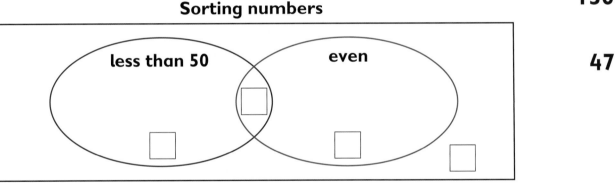

4 Copy the Venn diagram below.
Add the numbers to your diagram.

5 Count the numbers.
Write the totals in the squares.

6 a How many numbers have 3 tens?
  b How many numbers are odd?
  c How many numbers with 3 tens are odd?
  d Describe the numbers outside the sets.

27
24  10  31
38
30  65  8  53
20
34  17  40
22
37

**Sorting numbers**

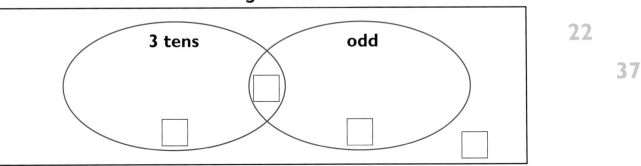

59

# Coin Carroll diagrams

## Refresher

Work in pairs.
You will need a 1p and a 2p coin.

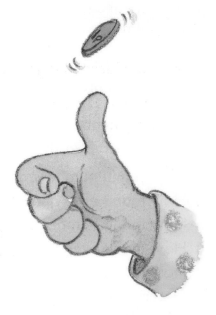

1  Copy the Carroll diagram.

2  Flip one coin 20 times.
   Make a cross in the Carroll diagram for each flip.

3  a  How many heads did you get?
      Write the number in the circle on the Carroll diagram.
   b  How many tails did you get?
      Write the number in the circle on the Carroll diagram.

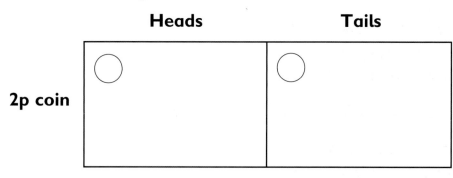

|  | **Heads** | **Tails** |
|---|---|---|
| **1p coin** | ○ | ○ |

4  Make a Carroll diagram for the other coin.

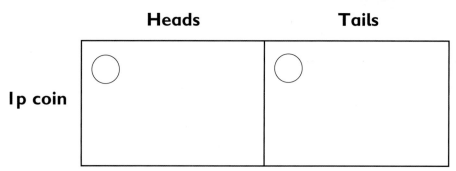

|  | **Heads** | **Tails** |
|---|---|---|
| **2p coin** | ○ | ○ |

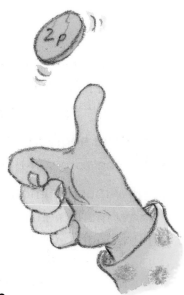

5  a  Which came up most: heads or tails?
   b  What is the difference between the number of heads and tails?

6  Look at both Carroll diagrams.
   a  Which coin came up heads most?
   b  How many tails were there altogether?
   c  Were there more heads or tails altogether?

## Practice

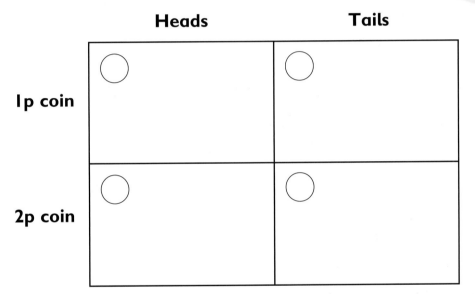

1  Copy the Carroll diagram.

2  Flip both coins together.
   Do this 20 times.

3  Make a cross in the Carroll diagram for each turn.

4  Write the number of crosses in each circle.

|          | **Heads** | **Tails** |
|----------|-----------|-----------|
| **1p coin** | ◯ | ◯ |
| **2p coin** | ◯ | ◯ |

5  a  Which coin got most heads?
   b  How many more heads than the other coin?
   c  How many heads were there altogether?
   d  How many tails were there altogether?

6  a  Flip the coins 20 times again and make a new Carroll diagram.

7  a  Did you get more tails the first or second time?
   b  Which coin showed the most tails altogether?
   c  How many tails were there for both coins altogether?

8  Make a third Carroll diagram to show all your results.

# Game Carroll diagrams

## Refresher

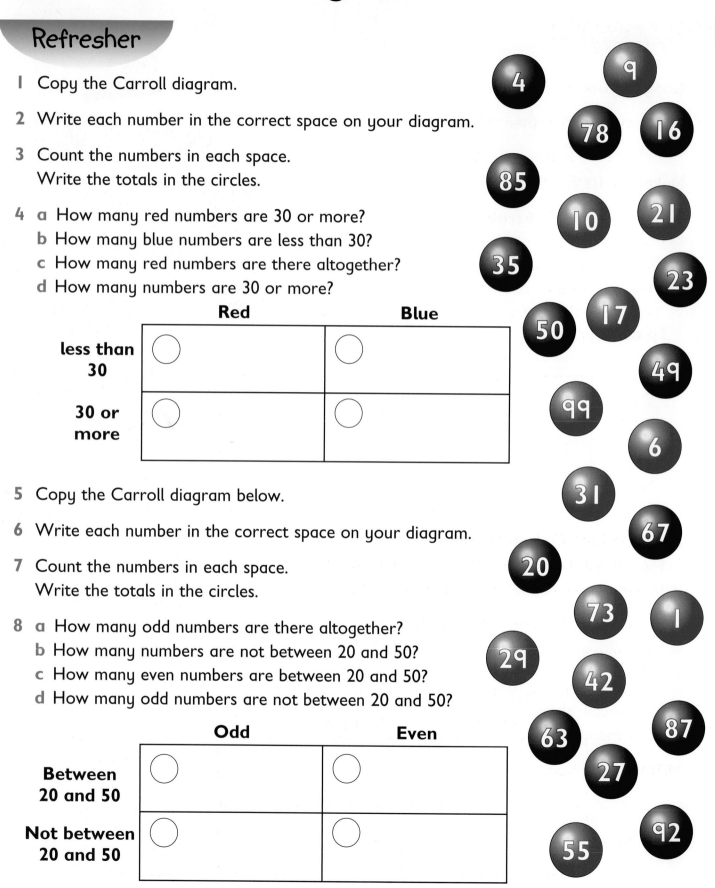

1  Copy the Carroll diagram.

2  Write each number in the correct space on your diagram.

3  Count the numbers in each space.
   Write the totals in the circles.

4  a  How many red numbers are 30 or more?
   b  How many blue numbers are less than 30?
   c  How many red numbers are there altogether?
   d  How many numbers are 30 or more?

|  | Red | Blue |
|---|---|---|
| **less than 30** | ◯ | ◯ |
| **30 or more** | ◯ | ◯ |

5  Copy the Carroll diagram below.

6  Write each number in the correct space on your diagram.

7  Count the numbers in each space.
   Write the totals in the circles.

8  a  How many odd numbers are there altogether?
   b  How many numbers are not between 20 and 50?
   c  How many even numbers are between 20 and 50?
   d  How many odd numbers are not between 20 and 50?

|  | Odd | Even |
|---|---|---|
| **Between 20 and 50** | ◯ | ◯ |
| **Not between 20 and 50** | ◯ | ◯ |

62

## Practice

This domino has the sum 2 + 5 = 7

1 Copy the Carroll diagram.

2 Write each sum in the correct space on your diagram.

3 Count the sums in each space.
Write the totals in the circles.

4 a How many red dominoes have an odd total?
  b How many dominoes with an even total are blue?
  c How many red dominoes are there?
  d How many dominoes have an even total?
  e Which are there more of: even or odd totals?
    How many more?

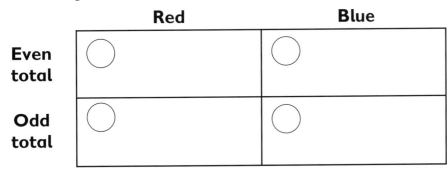

|  | Red | Blue |
|---|---|---|
| **Even total** | ◯ | ◯ |
| **Odd total** | ◯ | ◯ |

5 Copy the Carroll diagram below. Write each domino in the correct space on your diagram. Count the dominoes in each space. Write the totals in the circles.

This domino is a double

6 a How many dominoes are not doubles?
  b How many dominoes do not have a 6?
  c How many dominoes with a double have a six?
  d How many dominoes have a 6 but are not doubles?

This domino has a 6

This domino does not have a 6

|  | Has a 6 | Does not have a 6 |
|---|---|---|
| **Double** | ◯ | ◯ |
| **Not double** | ◯ | ◯ |

● Solve a problem by collecting quickly, organising, representing and interpreting data in tables, charts, graphs and diagrams, including those generated by a computer, for example: Venn and Carroll diagrams (two criteria)

Su 12, 5

# Travel diagrams

## Refresher

Some children in Class 4 wrote down how they travel to school and how far.

|  | **Walk** | **Do not walk** |
|---|---|---|
| **Travel less than 1 km** | ◯ | ◯ |
| **Travel 1 km or more** | ◯ | ◯ |

| | | |
|---|---|---|
| Jon | bus | $\frac{3}{4}$ km |
| Azul | car | 4 km |
| Kay | walk | $\frac{1}{4}$ km |
| Siren | bike | $1\frac{1}{4}$ km |
| Rabi | walk | $1\frac{1}{2}$ km |
| Mark | car | 10 km |
| Leon | walk | 1 km |
| Sid | bike | $\frac{1}{2}$ km |
| George | bus | $2\frac{1}{4}$ km |
| Bao Bao | bus | $3\frac{1}{2}$ km |
| Aaron | walk | 2 km |
| Poppy | walk | $\frac{1}{2}$ km |
| Colleen | car | 2 km |
| June | bus | 3 km |
| Hal | walk | $1\frac{1}{4}$ km |
| Allan | train | 5 km |
| Fiona | walk | $\frac{3}{4}$ km |
| Sophie | walk | $\frac{1}{4}$ km |
| Gavin | car | $\frac{1}{2}$ km |

1  Copy the Carroll diagram.

2  Write the children's names to show how they travel to school.

3  Write the totals in the circles.

4  a  How many children walk less than 1 km to school?

   b  How many children do not walk to school?

   c  How many children travel more than 1 km?

   d  How many children are in Class 4?

## Practice

1  Copy and complete the Venn diagram.

2  a  How many children do not walk to school and travel more than 1 km?

   b  How many children walk to school?

   c  How many children walk less than 1 km to school?

**How class 4 travel to school**

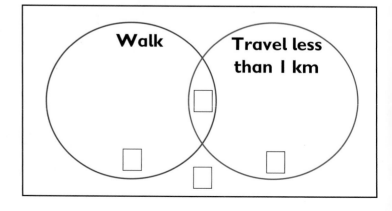

64